Very Eyes

Poems

Sid Gold

Poets' Choice

Poets' Choice Publishing

Cover Art: "Circle Game," by Sid Gold, 12" x 12," Acrylic & Pastel

Cover Design: Sanket Patel
Illustrations: Sid Gold
Photos of illustrations: Resa Moran
Graphic Design: Sanket Patel

Tom Kirlin, Editor

Printed in the United States of America

Library of Congress Control Number: 2023940798
ISBN 978-1-7371653-2-3

First Edition

Permission received for previously published poems.
Artist's permission granted for artwork.

Poets' Choice Publishing
Avery Heights, Suite 126
300 Brandegee Avenue
Groton, CT 06340
Poets-Choice.com
marathonfilm@gmail.com

Acknowledgments

Journals:

Backbone Mountain Review: "Animals," "Big Dogs," "Breeze," "Bribe," "Dialing Direct," "Hazards," "New Moon," "Perfect Day," "Poverty," "Sentinels," "Taking Off"

Broadkill Review: "Aubade," "Season of the Rat," "Storm Warnings"

Gargoyle: "Aleph," "Cry," "Beauty," "Dance," "Defeat," "Eyes," "Fit," "Hop"

Loch Raven Review: "A Litany" (as "Given"), "Another Nut," "Nothing," "The Light," "Waterman"

One Art: "In Country," "My L.A.," "Walking"

Maryland Literary Review: "Human Song," "The Odds"

Stone Poetry Quarterly: "Lucky Lucky Me," "Winter Song"

Schuylkill Valley Journal: "All Wet"

This Is What America Looks Like: The Washington Writers' Publishing House Anthology: "Absence"

Thank You
To Richard Harteis, Tom Kirlin, Resa Moran and Barbara Shaw for their help in bringing *Very Eyes* to fruition.

Table of Contents

Introduction
Tom Kirlin

Sid Gold opens his fifth book of poems with two youthful songs. "Taking Off" speaks of "speeding toward a bright star / we struggled to name, [when] we heeded / no voices, no counsel, but our own." "Dialing Direct" distills love to the heart's core, when: "all that remains audible / is the echoing of my pulse / racing, racing toward you." Then, abruptly, we wake to "Hills," a prose poem as flat as Kansas. It's scintillating opening line? "Some stories have a more specialized functions than do others."

Chaos ensues. A civic voice announces that President Nixon's motorcade was spat on in Caracas, that Bedouin tribesmen often shout "at one another even if sitting only a few feet apart," then demands we decide between "Weasel or wastrel? Sequence or sequins?" This witty dialectic is followed, midpoint in the poem, by the literary critic's dispassionate observation that "Anderson's fiction, however, underwent a favorable reappraisal throughout the Fifties."

Meanwhile, a dark political voice gains focus and force behind the cultured and socially observant ones noted above. That darkness hovers throughout the book; its foundation is laid in "Hills," whose second line is the ominous "The authorities, of course, suppressed all attempts at accurate cartography." Gold's concerns with political oppression, distortion and corruption are expressed indirectly: "The claims of occultists often ignore the rudiments of evidence," "They could appreciate, although rarely enjoy, the passing scene," "They believed in *thrift* but not in *savings*," and "Any small gathering, secret or not, may become a conspiracy." A shadowy world of emigrees emerges here, moving behind these lines. We glimpse, too, the poet's interest in making sense of these ancestral events and stories.

But most of all, by this third poem of *Very Eyes*, we know we are in erudite, ironic, capable hands. And so we are. Gold alternates between public and private voices, between lyric song and what I call faux-failed sonnets. On their surface, his prose poems appear to be the scrambled ramblings of a Mad Hatter, a persona anxious to make sense of this world and family history but apparently unable to do so. His narrator is obsessed with trivia and folk wisdom, burdened with everyday grief and extraordinary trauma, aware of social upheaval and issues like poverty—yet eager to share everyday reflections and advice on hygiene, literary criticism, war, philosophy, etiquette, the neighbor next door. There's fun to be had here, but attention must be paid.

Pronouns are extremely important in Gold's prose poems, as are tense and tone, perhaps never more so than in "Hills." Stylistically, the poet strikes a mock Hemingwayesque—or Robert Louis Stevenson?—pose in the final quatrain, one that evokes the poem's title:

> The musty smell of dust & acacia leaves
> under the hot sun. Such sacred mysteries, I must conclude aren't
> intended for everyone. The river, nonetheless, remains the
> river; & the hills—the lush, ripe green hills—remain the hills.

Once you've read the book, you realize this poem reveals the approximate decade the poet became aware of public events and heard stories of his ancestors fleeing Eastern Europe. He here presents his aesthetic: he will not shout, scatter sequins at our feet, suppress facts or ask us to believe in the occult. His rivers of emotion and thought will accurately flow, the colors will be vivid, the hills will remain hills no matter how scrambled they may at first appear.

Gold's lyric poems are equally rewarding, and more easily traversed. Take:

My LA

You don't have to love L.A.,
but you have to the love idea of it,
where the average Joe & Josephine's
hyper-realism meets the mundane,
America's off-kilter vision
of business-as-usual passing
momentarily for a happening scene

& all of those highways—named *free*
as if anything really is—going
in any direction you could point to.

He wakes in the morning

At a sprawling beach party
lit by bonfires. …. This is my L.A.,
I decided, flashing my best
newcomer's smile at everyone
who passed, to do with what I wish.

As the traveler moves east to west and back again, matures from youth to a golden age, he dispels illusion along the way. Emotions come into focus and are leeched away, sometimes literally. In "Human Song," when he cuts himself while shaving and sees blood start

clotting on my neck like a birthmark
I cannot help but venture a tentative smile
at the unmistakable humanity
minted like a coin upon my face.

His stubbornness meets its match in "Another Nut" when a squirrel "turned / his dark eye on us like a gunsight / & cracked another nut." More ominous are the poems about war and cultural extermination, such as in "Promises," which opens with "During winter, wolves survive mainly by scavenging carcasses" and end with "Only endure the night's broken promises."

The titles of poems alone tell the ambition of the work: Beauty, Hazards, Everything, Nothing, Animals, Angels, Bribe, Defeat, Tears, Poverty, Dancing, Promises, Walking, Stillness, Speed, Sense, Pursuits, Real, Regret. And yet a number stand out, including "Sentinels," a lyric poem about a crow who represents so much more. Gold has associated the bird with Nazi concentration camp guards in several prior poems. Here, the poet and the bird are evenly matched, guarding an apartment block where he lives:

> the single crow, its glossy wings
> a perfect machine, rose & alighted
> on a drainpipe while I remained
> attentively in place, wide-eyed, mute
> as a mannequin, just where it had
> fixed me, sentinels, the both of us,
> guarding a turning world.

The world knows "Defeat:" "Who among us, even in jest, has not spoken of defeat?" where "Concepts of beauty are of limited historical significance" (Ibid). A world that urges the poet to ask, as Gold does, in "Very Very:"

Cannot desire & progress coexist? Will not
a quick peek at a novel object engender
inner peace? Might not a sharpster,
slick as black ice on a two-lane, utilize
his sleight-of-hand to cause a shiny bauble
to vanish before our very very eyes?

To those who pay proper attention, Sid Gold's Very Eyes will not vanish
quickly from mind or heart. Or eyes. Keep it handy. This book is well
worth reading more than twice.

Tom Kirlin
Recipient, William Meredith Award in Poetry

TAKING OFF

We took off, the 396 crooning
its crude & bawdy tune, our mischief
the only jests we knew.

It was dusk, the sky streaked
like a week-old bruise, the ditches
rotten with rainwater. The high weeds,
grown tall enough to shelter
any fugitive, waved as we drove past
but we ignored them, ignored
the mute eyes staring from the dark woods,
ignored whoever stared blankly
from the windows of every lone homestead.

Roaring with youth, the night air
spiced with moonlight, our blood shimmered
like raw silk. A single true act of courage,
we believed, would redeem all sins
& speeding toward a bright star
we struggled to name, we heeded
no voices, no counsel, but our own.

SECTION I

DIALING DIRECT

Years of agreeing
on so little until we've come
to agree on this:
long-distance conversation
is a leash so long
& unforgiving the choke-collar
at its terminus seems
all the more cruel.

At times, I admit,
all that remains of you
is your voice, a keen stylus
of current inscribing
the journal of your seasons
on recall's photosensitive screen:
a few breathy strokes
of speech—hesitant, tender,
carping, bold—your various aspects
imprinted for safekeeping
in a single heart's archives
by an aural code.

Listen to what I say now:
you are the live wire
threaded through my inner ear,
coiled around my heart.
Cut the juice
& all that remains audible
is the echoing of my pulse
racing, racing toward you.

HILLS

Some stories have a more specialized function than do others. The
authorities, of course, suppressed all attempts at accurate cartography.
And yet Nixon's motorcade was spat upon while moving slowly
through Caracas. Early safes were merely wooden strongboxes & easily
disassembled. Becoming overwhelmed by all that color, she determined,
isn't a bad idea. The Bedouin habitually shouted at one another even
if sitting only a few feet apart. Faber had received permission to rattle
that cage whenever he desired. The claims of occultists often ignore
the rudiments of evidence. Only squares, while triangles were called
for. In the distance, a herd of oryx looking very white against the dark
plain. Weasel or wastrel? Sequence or sequins? They could appreciate,
although rarely enjoy, the passing scene. They believed in thrift, but not
in savings. *No sé decirte cómo fue.* The fever of their ambition was not
my own. Anderson's fiction, however, underwent a favorable reappraisal
throughout the Fifties. Any small gathering, secret or not, may become a
conspiracy. The musty smell of dust & acacia leaves under the hot sun.
Such sacred mysteries, I must conclude, aren't intended for everyone.
The river, nonetheless, remains the river; & the hills—the lush, ripe green
hills—remain the hills.

ABSENCE

I left the apartment
just once, a few moments
past dawn, saw all
was unchanged & returned.

Day long the landing
was a way station, the still air
shivering with each passing,
each coming & going
proclaimed in a private tongue.

And yet whenever
I looked out, nothing,
the blank walls unseeing,
a single light fixture
keeping its secrets to itself.

I wonder whether my neighbors
are like me: watchful
at the thought of catastrophe,
suspicious in its absence.

SUNRISE

Bloom mistrusted the prevailing scholarship on Shakespeare's politics. Yet one should practice good hygiene in a copper mine. Failing to keep track of the exact date has little to do with fate. I wanted the *brasas*, but not the *pollo*. Are you too easily distracted by trivia? Not everything you need will fit into an expensive handbag. The mountain itself was benign, but its color was quite hostile. Anyone at all can be held tightly in a dream. Oh, to be caught up in a temporal wake. Atget, it turns out, was a surprisingly good businessman. That day, the agony of multitudes blackened the skies. Image, but not homage. Prance, but not prince. She can be clever as hell, noted a voice across the room, if she wants to be. It is important that we agree on the medium of exchange. Although being overcome by a pyroclastic cloud invariably proves fatal. You could call that sunrise tangerine smear; the risen sun, chrome yellow.

MY L.A.

You don't have to love L.A.,
but you have to love the idea of it,
where the average Joe & Josephine's
hyper-realism meets the mundane,
America's off-kilter vision
of business-as-usual passing
momentarily for a happening scene

& all those highways—named *free*
as if anything really is—going
in any direction you could point to.
The goal is to get there—somewhere,
anywhere—faster than is reasonable
& expecting acclaim or a prize
for your efforts is energy wasted.

I was there once, hitchhiking in
from a stretch posing as a tourist
in the badlands east of Eden.
I landed somehow in Pasadena,
where I sidled into a silvery Stingray,
its owner a tanned poster child
for the middle-aged good life,
& felt enobled without even trying.
I was looking for Venice, the address
scrawled on my wrist, & ready
for all kinds of surprises
found it nothing close to home.

But that's the point, someone said
at a sprawling beach party
lit by bonfires. It wasn't being given
for me & the next morning, the coals
still glowing, revelers struggled
to recall how they got there
& with whom. This is my L.A.,
I decided, flashing my best
newcomer's smile at everyone
who passed, to do with what I wish.

BEAUTY

Feral animals generally dislike being stared at or approached directly. Certainly, Harriman noted, all children should be taught to share. Yet no one could have predicted the public's responsiveness to Pop Art. Are we not always distracted by expectation? The small bridge in Arnéguy serves as the border between Spain & France. Put those warm boots on quickly, she commanded, before I change my mind. Trane's early passing was indicated by Pluto in the Fifth House. The blinding glitter of the bay at rest. Cleanse, but not clench. Mystery, but not enigma. Some trees remain silent about their aspirations. Some trees are friendlier to strangers than others. *Mit diesem Kerlis nichts sie machen.* You know, the teased hair, the melting lipstick, the skirts up to here. The term now in favor is Opioid Use Disorder. Entire landscapes may be transformed in a matter of minutes. At his best, Powell could solo inventively no matter how demanding the tempo. My father is a notably patient man, he threatened. I, however, am not. If not leisure, at least a few hours of silence. Does it really matter, in the end, where beauty is found?

HAZARDS

Today a stray cat lays squashed
against the asphalt, its belly split
& spilling like the meat of a strange fruit,
its entrails jellied in the heat.

Drawing closer, we search
for a sign, some mark signifying loss
or deliverance. And though a shadow
closes about us, a twinge of conscience,
perhaps, for some deed thought
forgotten, we know it as nothing more
than a plump raincloud darkening the air.

Still, if we wish, all may be seen anew:
the road, the vanished automobile, ourselves,
the commonplaces of life re-cast.

And if some of us are given to prayer,
we may say something near us dies
& through its passing is transfigured,
a road sign signaling hazards up ahead.

EVERYTHING

The waste chemicals of cocaine production have long polluted
Colombia's waters. Their interrogators, they noticed, made a point of
blocking the light. Stevens was notably reluctant to preserve drafts of
his work. Although salty sweets are quite popular in Nordic countries.
With those who assumed such privileges, I had scant patience. Tornadoes
arrive by land; hurricanes, by sea. That the materials will slowly degrade
is part of the process. Not promote, but promise. Not usurp, but upset. Hit
lever tendered fly blind. Nevertheless, she relished running the occasional
red light. Such clues may imply a number of outcomes. As soil rich
in iron is not well-suited for agriculture. Hence, the Crow mounted
war parties even in the depths of winter. Boogie or boggle? Function
or faction? That expansive manner is doubtlessly a stall tactic. Rush
hour traffic stuttering along like a line of herded steers. Not everything,
Adelaide reminded him patiently, must always add up.

HUMAN SONG

How strange to have come all this way
on the path toward perfect ignorance
& to have stopped here, a man alone

in his hair shirt, incarnate among those
who scoff at fate & enjoy rough games
& luck they never comprehend.

How different to have been a goat—
surefooted, obstinate—but keeping
my mouth shut when undisturbed

or a cicada, sleeping away the years
& content to wait patiently for the chance
to pitch my wingsong into an electric blur.

Each morning, when I seek my daemon
in the mirror above the sink, a strawberry
of fresh blood drawn by a dull blade

clotting on my neck like a birthmark
I cannot help but venture a tentative smile
at the unmistakable humanity
minted like a coin upon my face.

FIT

For Richard Peabody

Blavasky's adherents, for example, believed she had achieved
transcendence. By then, you understand, every word spoken was a
gamble. A few pigmy crocodiles lazily watched us with unblinking
yellow eyes. The wind in the elms caressing the silence. Filling in the
blanks, Eliza boasted immodestly, is my forte. Leavis carried a slim
volume of Milton's poems with him on the Western Front. Dada is
useless, exulted Tzara. Photorealist painting, however, generally depicts
mundane subject matter. Yet only one species of confession was found
relevant. Specimen or spectacle? Review or revile? A gentleman saves
his bawdy tales for the smoking room. A gentleman does not greet
strangers as *Pal*. How I do it, she winked, is my own little secret. Joselito
succumbed from his wounds following his fourth goring in the bull ring.
And now their modest scheme had come to a sudden end. *La notte e
vicina por me.* It is impossible, it was said, to live in Los Angeles forever.
The term *romantic* should never be limited solely to amorous pursuits.
Save me, he pleaded. Save me from a suit that doesn't fit.

IN COUNTRY

Driving the two-lane,
its white line a beacon,
half-past midnight in country
you don't know, the radio spouting
hard-shell sermons & static,
you can't wait

for the next town,
the gabled homes set back
from the street, their wide verandahs
dim as grottos, & the convergence
& split of the high roads
at the town square, the lone stoplight
flashing an angry red.

You've been waiting—
prepared, in fact—for the small
yet welcome surprises—a roadhouse,
shaking with noise & lit up
for a holiday with no beginning
or end, its gravel lot an OK Corral
of pick-ups & Harleys.

I am ready for anything,
you think, having come this far,
but in truth nothing more
is happening, nothing
but you & the high beams
moving forward, eyes
on the road, a fish out of water
in the liquid dark of night.

THAT

The feathers are ruffled. Whose? Another mystery for the misbegotten.
It's a rare bird that returns to its captor. Yet that bridge was crossed
& crossed yet again until none recalled when they had arrived or left.
Casting the fishing line between tragedy & comedy. You want to tell
the tale, but the words tell another, a story long in the mucking. Make
up, children, play nice. Time burning like a kerosene-drenched wick.
We thought the drumming would never cease. A headache not worth the
awkwardness. You can be certain no one asks me to translate. Safety
off when entering the theater of conflict. The moon with its 150-proof
shine. Although a long walk in the woods may lead almost anywhere.
What Haims needs is a better reason to get up in the morning. A tightly
woven pattern of lawn ornaments. All kinds of mayhem, but not that
sort. Stinking drunk, we decided. And packing heat in a steamer trunk.
I'm breaking out the good stuff, she announced, flashing that honeydew
smile. A storm coming up down the road. My good friend, dozing pie-
faced as a pumpkin. And what they'd said earlier. All of that.

NEW MOON

Across the way
the old bungalow
sits empty as a skull.

She was born there,
refused doctor's advice,
died there.

Two years later
her daughters
still shake their heads.

All reasons,
explanations,
down the storm drain.

Months pass,
insistent as logic.

At the new moon
a sleek raccoon, serene
as a mogul, sidles around
the corner, its snout raised

& alert for the scent
of carrion, the sly odors
of spoilage, a slow but steady rot.

DANCE

Extra riders on a sled increases the likelihood of someone's falling off.
A border should signify more than a uniformed man holding a gun.
Her eyes had become, for the moment, a languid green, yet cold as the
sea. Readers belatedly came to appreciate Lawrence's vividly charged
language. That's beauty enough for me right there, he said, pointing. The
light of understanding has made me most discreet. Nearby a few small
cannon lay half-buried in the dried mud. Sunset, but not Sun Yat-Sen.
Squint, but not squid. Christianity had found its way to Celtic Britain by
the second century. Casey's moods can be quite amphibious, she warned
before leaving. Our laziness, we agreed, was not necessarily a handicap.
The glossary listed at least thirty-two distinct artistic movements. Hauling
ash will never be mistaken for a picnic. That accent may be described
as hard-edged. Egyptian obelisks were hewn from single blocks of
stone. Although one's ability to resist Celia's bright smile is imperative.
Originally, temporal power belonged to a perpetual priesthood. Surely,
the two-fisted approach has its obvious drawbacks. Invade or invent?
Prevalent or prescient? Isn't celibate a kind of fish?, asked the attendant.
Something that occurs frequently, but never in German. It becomes
difficult, over time, to neglect our necessary enemies. All that hot
comedy. All that glittering dance.

NOTHING

Kindness alone cannot save
the world. What other tragedy—
large or small—is there?, I ask
myself as I help an elderly woman
move some boxes, a bit more

of a task, I must admit, than
I bargained for. You are so kind,
she says, by way of thanks. And
don't tell me it's nothing, she adds.
Nothing you do is nothing.

ALEPH

The pattern of folds in the cerebrum differs in every individual. Evergood rejected abstraction in order to express his socialist ideals. Demons, Katy concluded, come in all shapes & hues. Preserved kernels of wheat have been found in Stone Age storage pits. Tomato & chocolate are Aztec; angry & glitter are Norse. We were drunk much of the time; not most, but much. Dodging reduces the density of a photograph's dark areas. If nothing else, we can ignore progress. Wonder, but not wander. Torment, but not torture. Ask yourself whether ink is truly your friend, advised Becca. The Olympian gods were often capricious in their dealings with humans. Rust, for example, is a common form of electrochemical corrosion. Pushkin & Lermontov died in duels; Yessinin & Mayakovsky were suicides. One doesn't witness a bus tipping over very often. The gentle art of behaving gently. Seconds are bound to seek a reconciliation prior to the meeting. At the time, capitalism was thought to be a progressive advancement. A sliderule is not a slipper. A detonator is not a deodorant. I promise, vowed Mikayla, to maintain your interest. Surely, there is a road somewhere in the middle, as flat & straight as any road might be. Armed skirmishes were fought along the Amur River for several decades. Verily, is there another like Imhotep? It was suggested Clayton save that tidbit for some other picnic. No warning shots fired, read the sign. The camel is *gimmel*; the house is *beth*; and the ox—the sturdy, broad-horned ox—is *aleph*.

PERFECT TIME

The air in the parking lot
at midnight is clear & black.
It's fine for standing still & breathing,
the temperature dropping
just enough to tickle bare skin.

Otherwise, there is no good reason
to remain—alone, my breath
even as a second hand—
other than the world seems
to have come to rest for a moment
& all is hushed as a passing thought.

An occasion to do nothing
as should, according
to Wang Wei, the serious man.

How could have I known
this is the perfect time
to enter my life?

LEAVES

Numerous spice roads were established during the Bronze Age. Luckily, some bright percussion arrived just in time. Making sense, thought Faber, may be coincidental. While sharpshooters normally qualify at a distance of six-hundred feet. Of course they were lying, but no one really minded. The tiger's muscles rippling effortlessly beneath its stripes. Not mask, but musk. Not piecemeal, but permissible. Will we ever adjust to the new China? Now emperor, Trajan declared himself Jupiter's earthly representative. A heart beating like the thrashing of a hooked fish. On that trip, common lichen was usually called f*ur. Marche lentement dans le matin endormi.* Always strive to appear good-humored, counseled Haims. That day, no stern grandmothers netted crawdaddies from the river. Yet any one of various dead languages will urge you toward heaven. The reassurance of early light in autumn. The crisp, dry leaves turning ceaselessly in the wind.

ALL WET

You think about how or what it
might have been, but does it matter?
It may rain. It may not. Regardless,
all wet is a condition to consider.
Who, you ask, talks like that anyway?
Not anyone grumbling *sotto voce*
on the checkout line at the Save-A-Lot.
We all have other things on our minds
& keep most of them, thankfully,
to ourselves. At times someone else—
another personage, you might say—
is actually listening, grateful as all
getout your problems, your issues,
are nothing resembling their own.
Luck could just be a lady, if you
know what, within limits, I mean.
In the parking lot, so many cars
look alike. Not really, but we prefer
to see them that way. It's a trick
of the eye intended to forestall envy
& other resentments. Tell the truth now,
you think of telling, commanding,
a woman stuffing bags of whatnot
into the trunk of a waxed Corolla.
She's already given you a quick glance.
Humanoid, apparently, is the verdict
& you prefer to believe you're harmless,
at least as things go, & dry enough
to appear in public on good days.
It has rained, you discover, exiting

the store, & everything—the asphalt,
pitted, veined with cracks, the painted
metal, the tiny islands of foliage—
is all wet, everything, that is, but you.
I refuse to drown today, you promise,
searching the sky for an angry cloud
with your name on it & finding none,
glory in your state. The non-drowner,
that's me, you privately exult while
about you all—the world we tell our-
selves we know—remains submerged.

NUMBERS

There are varieties of vertigo that have little to do with losing consciousness. In Mexico, for instance, more than one-hundred million butterflies took flight. No, his playing did not sound at all *academic*. Is that how we're thinking about copper today?, she asked gently. They did a better job, fortunately, with glassware. One may play games, but not always in groceries. In those days, he was told, the Panamanians lived down on Lafayette Street. Not sinking, but descending. Not drinking, but imbibing. A plain earthenware bowl pulsing from the hand that shaped it. The Privy Council urged the young Elizabeth Tudor to marry immediately. Although fiery blazes will travel anywhere they choose. Bruno, for a change, appeared distracted, but harmless. Let us see what happens next, was another suggestion. Crystallized, it is crystal. Yet Attila, the Scourge of God, died of natural causes at forty-six. Oh, so many wagons, so many wheels. You don't know the numbers. The numbers don't know you.

"Mirage"

8" x 8", Acrylic & Pastel

29

"Destination #1"

4" x 4", Acrylic & Pastel

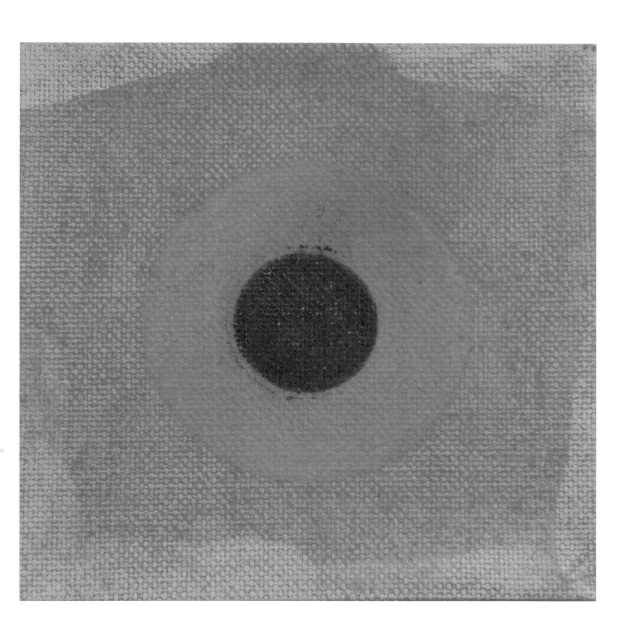

"Twin Moons #1"

7" x 7", Acrylic & Pastel

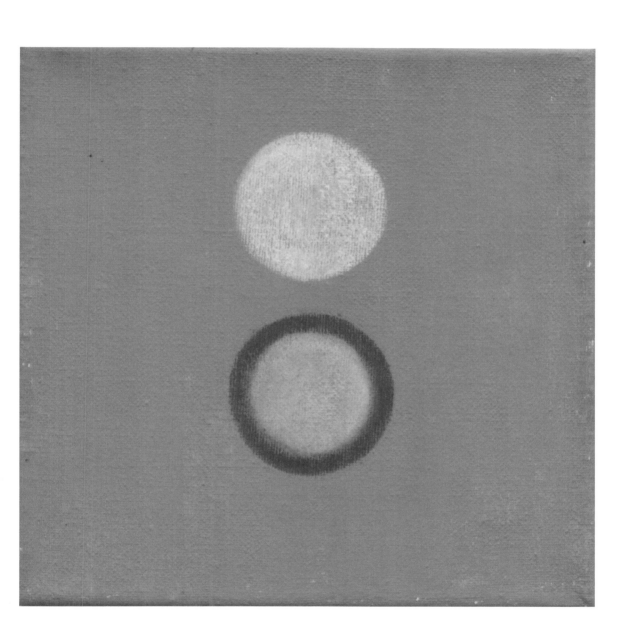

"Distance"

10" x 8", Acrylic

SECTION II

ANOTHER NUT

At dusk we sat on the lawn,
unblinking as toads, as darkness
poured through the cradle
of our arms like ink, the night
settling over us like a flat stone.
Nothing visible moved.
The least gesture may have
shattered even a distant star.
And soon a litany of fears—poverty,
blindness, dying alone & unloved—
emerged on the grass one
by one like squirrels, their jaws
gnawing at acorns held
in their paws like worry beads,
poised to scatter to the periphery
of our vision where all we perceive
is a flutter, shadow assuming
the shape of thought.
Growing edgy, we tossed a pebble
or two & watched them scamper:
all but one, who hopped
a few yards distant, turned
his dark eye on us like a gunsight
& cracked another nut.

BRIBE

Managing fire effectively was *Homo Erectus'* most lasting achievement.
At first, Howl appeared to escape prosecution. Nonetheless, Giacometti's
attenuated figures express vulnerability & despair. I can sit here all
day long, bristled Furman, but not like a sack. The stark & puritanical
noonday sun in August. And yet it was easy to grasp for straws in a
hayfield. For the diving tarantula is no ordinary spider. *No sé explicarme
qué pasó*. Paradise or paradox? Donate or donut? Iceland's citizenry
still numbers fewer than 400,000. The past, it is rumored, is a strange &
wondrous country. Tall buildings much prefer properly poured concrete.
Tall buildings don't care whether they are in the way. Kerouac soon
learned to refrain from smoking hashish laced with arsenic. While incest
taboos, though they may vary, are universal. Something soothing, but not
obviously Scandinavian. Originality, however, was not a virtue on that
occasion. The scenario required a tree, at least one, & some shade. How
large a bribe, he inquired politely, will be sufficient?

ANGRY BEAST

A neighbor is spending his morning
under his red Dodge pick-up.
He has help. That's not the problem.
It's hard to ignore a working man
at work at a job out in the open
& so, curious as any cat, you pause
to watch. In short order, he curses softly,
closes his eyes, gathers himself,
& wrist & forearm readied, works
that wrench. His buddies, hovering
like maiden aunts, nod encouragement
while glancing at their watches.
Everyone wants this done before the heat
rises like water boiling in a saucepan.
Everyone wants a cold sixpack or two.
You've been there yourself, more
than once, under a derelict vehicle.
Hearing it start—that exhaust firing up
like an angry beast—is a music all its own.

ANIMALS

Iroquois longhouses were built to shelter a number of related families. Might not a hot, dry wind blow away all foreboding? I am always interested in mature content, revealed Vivian. Yet fully one-fifth of Europe's wildlife is threatened with extinction. If asked, the typical audience prefers not to be confused. As even the executioner must return home for dinner. Flamenco, says the guidebook, did not originate with the Romani. Nearly all poolroom spectators, however, are potential opponents. Mesquite or mosquito? Eunuch or unique? They had heard the sound in the distance & strained to hear it more clearly. While the night sky claims certain privileges. Some trees believe mobility is overrated. Some trees lack the common social graces. She soon learned to recognize sundown habits wherever they appeared. There are ways legislators can protect vital segments of the workforce, protested Eubanks. In short, one set of kettle drums will usually suffice. The sun's oblique glare buttering the horizon. *This is not Wonderland,* announced the bright letters on the warehouse wall. Nonetheless, most animals will consume their food where they find it.

LUCKY LUCKY ME

Once, not long ago, Linda Gregg spoke
of white crows. They inhabited her world,
a blasted, untamed landscape she conjured up
for us, her willing believers. Some would have
gladly become her acolytes, but she had
none of it. She went it alone, criss-crossing
the land with a voice stolen from a ghost,
confident most mistook it for death,
the death we've learned to expect some
unnamed day. I've searched for those crows.
White, I've decided, is an easy color to hide
behind. Gregg also told us they were both
male & female. What else? Yet I'm thinking
those white crows are a third gender,
a savage, remorseless sex that drains life
from the eyes, bleaching the soul with their
remorseless, unwavering gaze. They are
happy creatures, happy crows, their caws
the voice of joy, at a pitch only crows can hear.
Common crows—*Corvus*, our lasting friends—
have no room for such joy in their lives.
I've searched, too, for the lambs she
mentioned, the chosen ones, to no avail.
I think now I will find them both—the white
crows, the chosen lambs—when the plague
now afflicting the lands to the north spreads
farther south. They'll congregate—in flocks,
in herds—in supermarket parking lots, chanting
Death, Death, Death in unison. And only I—
lucky, lucky me—will see & hear them.

PROMISES

During winter, wolves survive mainly by scavenging carcasses. A shaman's preparing medicines without prayer was believed unlucky. And of what specific use is an 18-inch brass rod? Afterward, Andre wept at the notion that Nadia was lost to him forever. Starfish—whether grilled or fried—are rarely served as a main dish. Nevertheless, McNamara ignored the misgivings of his aides while visiting Vietnam. He's much too adverbial for my taste, observed Kate's mother. As expensive forgeries will often evade easy detection. The unpredictable paths of butterflies in flight. Not London, but lowdown. Not Cairo, but cargo. Nailing it, Haims felt, was a harmless enough diversion. The contrast between Trane & Miles was essential to the Quintet's impact on its audience. All juices, without exception, are precipitates. The Vikings, it appears, rarely wore ornaments fashioned from gold. And yet we know almost nothing of Shakespeare's religion. *We shall live again,* chanted the Ghost Dancers in their fringed tunics. *We shall live again.* Only endure the night's broken promises.

WALKING

For Holly Karapetkova

Fortunately, you can go out walking.
You expect very little, only dusk
foreshadowing night, the murmur
of animal life at the ready, & a breeze,
its edge honed sharper than expected.
For now, solitude is desire without
fanfare. You can take stock, see things
for what they seem without the burden
of intellect or wit. You could explain
all this, make sense of it, if surrounded,
threatened, coaxed, enticed. Oh yes,
an audience—close friends or passersby,
lovers, perhaps—all suitably intrigued
enough to stick around. What could be
better? You might tell them the night
is yours alone & loneliness a form
of joy that doesn't advertise. They may
chuckle & swear they understand.
Yo comprendo, says one, as Spanish
is a loving tongue. *Do come with us,*
they urge, walking toward the bright
lights, your protests, heard as little other
than the rustle of dry leaves, of no use.

REGRET

Each night between six & seventeen dead bodies were discovered on the streets of Paris. The Old English term *wicca* was the equivalent of sorcerer. Dr. Glitter, however, resented being mistaken for a cat. At dawn, a young gull stood on the shoals, quietly eating its fill. The absolute but calming silence of the cosmos. Mather fils mistrusted certain evidence, yet he did nothing to stop the trials. Nevertheless, the Australian continent drifts slowly northward. Auden, claims Arendt, was neither vain nor humble. I much prefer to visit the second country on the list, she persisted. Radial, but not radical. Kinky, but not cranky. Claver me now, he spattled, for Tuesday is no dunce cloister. Sacred cows, no matter how indolent, are not the only livestock on the farm. I am so determined to mess with it, divulged Allison. While a lone locust easily consumes its weight each day. The basic structure of billiards will eliminate most attempts at cheating. The terrible mirror of the sky, empty of clouds. All that year they lived daringly & yet never came to regret any of it.

THE LIGHT

We know the story.
We tell it all the time.

The sun sets; the moon rises;
we search the skies for signs.

We see what we see
& each morning wake into ourselves,
remembering the night,
what it had to say.

Which of us, shrugging off
the passing of the hours
like a change of clothes

can forget the darkness,
the ready embrace of silence
at its edge, the fading of the light?

STILLNESS

An hereditary aristocracy, by definition, comprises a minority. Rodia mixed his own concoction of concrete to build his seventeen towers. Certainly, a text-based approach has its own rewards. We are all timid. And yes, we are all rash. Dixon disguised his Teutonic underpinnings quite successfully. Although most predators rely primarily on their sense of smell. The mid-summer fields whirring with heat. As Ursula's lips quivered in bewilderment. Bazaar & kiosk are Farsi; coffee & divan, Turkish. Acting or aching? Flamenco or flamingo? Neither of them questioned their notions of beauty. Quilted garments were rare in Europe until the twelfth century. A gentleman does not deface public notices. A gentleman resists sneezing into his sleeve. Yet the Crown of the Seven Crows is rarely worn in public. Optimistic accessories, thought Marcy, are the order of the day. His irascibility can be charming, she professed, but only at a distance. Trumball calls upon the memories of those who knew Fitzgerald intimately. The bland & cautious smiles of careful men. Contentment often generates its own surprises. Each object, nonetheless, is what it is intended to be. There, a stillness I no longer recognized.

SPEED

In the backlot a disabled roadster,
resplendent as a candy wrapper,
sleeps the sleep of a rotting log.

If asked, its owner will recount
his pricey coupe's past glories
like a greying, one-hit rock star
bragging about packed houses
in middling venues now defunct.
His mind's eye sees it whole again,
with speed enough to overtake
anyone's azure-skied fantasy
of the open road. He envisions
himself roaring down a two-lane,
a lone racer chasing nothing
but his rum notion of paradise
on a byway so lonely map-makers
cannot promise it exists.

Friends, accustomed to his rambling,
smile politely at these hot musings.
Guessing the fate of keepsakes
no longer worth keeping is a game
they no longer play. They say this—
without intending to offend—hoping
their neighbor will find a moment
to raise his foot off the throttle
of his desire & heed their good advice.

What he will do, they can guess,
is turn away & scowling like a tomcat
teased to distraction, kick a stone
toward a vague distance mirroring
his own conception of loss.
He would gladly kick the tires, too,
but they are already flat.

SENSE

With a rusty groan, the entire apparatus pivoted a quarter-turn southward. The Rashid were small, lean men, always watchful & alert. Recently, more worshippers than ever had been flocking to the sacred places. In the halls of the mighty, one must be prepared for anything. The development of the wheel paralleled the domestication of horses. And yet water is always the enemy of architecture. For now, I am more interested in non-existent conversations, explained Eve. A soft, calming rain blossoming in the nearby hills. The small, unforeseen pleasures of one's daily round. The Japanese, the class was informed, have a great respect for mirrors. An alloy's specific properties derive from its atomic structure. A syringe is not a sewing needle. A fishhook is not a friendship ring. All told, eighteen Romanovs ruled Russia. Scowling, his overcoat buttoned tight against the sudden chill. Her striking visage intoxicated us all. Hannibal, however, was undefeated until he wintered his troops at Capua. I know my heart, Rousseau insisted. And I know men. I beg you, my friend, make what little sense you can.

STORM WARNINGS

all night long

an unforgiving wind tells us
all we'd rather not know

PURSUITS

Onlookers often display an unlikely respect for drunken men. And yet a functioning pair of wings should come in handy. The day so bright you begin to doubt its sincerity. How many out-of-body experiences can an individual withstand? Blue sings in every voice. Black, unsurprisingly, can stand alone. I was thinking of Cranmer, of all people, & his prayer book. Who succeeds in eluding the grasp of the passing hours? Flames, she was assured, are not material objects. Waffle or woeful? Loathsome or lonesome? I do it to call attention to form, disclosed Faber. Nevertheless, the duties of capable bodyguards are inarguable. While the vibrations along the length of a taut string will produce a ground note. Attend to one's daily round, counseled the text, & its understated charms. No shenanigans: no gimmicks: no games. Friend, if you're going to Brownsville, stay on the right-hand road. There are many congenial pursuits available other than breaking & entering.

A LITANY

What we are given by parents:
the thick books with blank pages.

What we are given by teachers:
the vacant classrooms.

What we are given by employers:
the boxes of out-of-date files.

What we are given by friends:
the parting handshakes.

What we are given by lovers:
the faded photographs.

What we are given by day:
the loud knock on the door.

What we are given by night:
the empty mirror on the wall.

What we are given when alone:
the freshly-dug grave.

REAL

Effective renegotiation is merely one of many concerns. Chains, however, cannot help but be restrictive. Shall there be an unexpected dearth of cakes & ale? As the garments at runway shows are rarely offered for public sale. The dark, empty pavement like satin under the streetlights. All lasting societies must have their froth. Radish or ravish? Carapace or codpiece? There were women who hunted game. There were women who did not. Just think of the many places we might hide. Some distortion may be viewed as a necessary outcome. Yet Miranda refused to cherish keepsakes or past loves. Death's unforgiving fist. And that's what the moon is all about, he insisted. Nevertheless, ostentation is frequently shunned. What memory of the ashes & dust do we retain? You, too, may dance as fast as you can. That which mirrors do to the real.

WINTER SONG

For Jennifer Browne

In the half-death of winter,
a day whose only companions

are wind & ice, you might stand out
in the weather freezing & then freezing

even more, waiting for nothing other
than a deep chill to brittle your bones.

There is no good reason for this
but that the wind—stabbing, untamed,

predatory as a sabertooth—holds a truth
with a bite all its own, a truth, as it

happens, cursed as any dark omen.
Whatever it tells you, standing alone,

shivering & exposed, your breath frost,
there is little else to do but remain

where you are, watching the life you know
heave & buckle in the driving sleet.

ANGELS

Modigliani's death left Soutine with a horror of alcoholism. No, good people do not mind losing their way on occasion. A witness often believes he saw something he should not. That kingdom, we now know, is the realm of the Dark Prince. You fully intended to tell her, but conveniently forgot. Some trees can be quite stand-offish. Some trees prefer not to gossip among themselves. *Believe you me* willfully violates the rules of grammar. Moments before sunrise & the birds already stirring the day awake. Count them, the number of public buildings built by slave labor. Courteous or curious? Erection or election? Like a waterfall too insignificant to take seriously. One is not always required to be modernistic. While memory's bonfire rages alone. The silence was annoyingly shattered by a sudden reproof. Yet the majority of complaints lead to no corrective action. From above, a melody smooth & lush as velvet. You want to stick a sharper image in there, advised Faber. Ultimately, the Roman republic slid into tyranny. The bleached & bloodless bones of the past. Angels, whatever their guise, may be easily distracted.

AUBADE

I awoke just past dawn,
pillow-headed, the lamp still
burning from last night's read,
my neck a rusty hinge.

Then I remembered my dream
of loss, peopled by a cast
of former co-workers I barely knew.

Today, I promised,
I will love no one & no one,
nothing, shall love me in return.

CREATURE

Purple is the color of the girl's fear, explained Gauguin. There were reactions, but not responses. Will they hold up on the back end?, that's the question. That night, unfortunately, the moon was no use at all. Although people generally prefer others to dress neatly. She had often been told she was a pretty color. Soon the larvae will require all the energy they can muster. The traditional feel of exposed brick & earthenware tiles. Snug or snag? Ostrich or ostracize? Till then, no one had given much thought to Helsinki. Yet Akiva waited until his forties to begin serious study. Sitting patiently in a sidewalk cafe does not ensure a friend's timely arrival. Will romantic ideals survive industrialization? Once again, Haims begged off contributing to the narrative. Rodents, for example, are invariably relentless. One area of stress is the natural gas space. While all forms of exchange are based on shared trust. The unapologetic fictiveness of fiction. The reassuring lustre of fine silk under the fingertips. And finally, this creature who could not possibly be me.

SINGLE STAR

In the depths of night, let us each
open our eyes & search the sky
for that single star that is our own.

And if we find it, a distant nailhead
of light that shapes the darkness,
if it speaks to us in that tongue
we hear only as our inner voice

let us kneel, heads bowed, the noise
of living hushed as a held breath
& listen to that for which
we alone cannot find the words.

CONDOR

Dr. Johnson called for *conversation,* but Boswell persisted in *talking.* Despite their bulk, fully-grown bears are surprisingly agile. Her family was resentful, brooding & at times, violent. The dry winter sun muted in a cold, clear sky. It was a story he preferred not to hear, let alone think about. Moreover, moisture had seeped in there & soon a black mold appeared. Shyness when plaza. Refuse true hay mist. Tall buildings appreciate their views of nearby parks. Tall buildings must be prepared to withstand tornadoes. Somehow, the translators had omitted the parts about head lice. She glittered. And yes, she glowed. Placing patent leather items in a dustbag will prevent color migration. *Rosalie* is considered minor Porter, but it served Hines' purposes. Not super, but sober. Not renegade, but retrograde. By 1708, South Carolina had a majority Black population. Buddhism, in fact, does not recognize the authority of the Vedas. Everyone was so bleeping witty, yet in an understated way. Right now, she was assured, is when the fun begins. While over this vast wilderness, the Andean condor reigns supreme.

"Early Autumn"

12" x 16", Acrylic

"Twin Moons #2"

4" x 4", Acrylic & Pastel

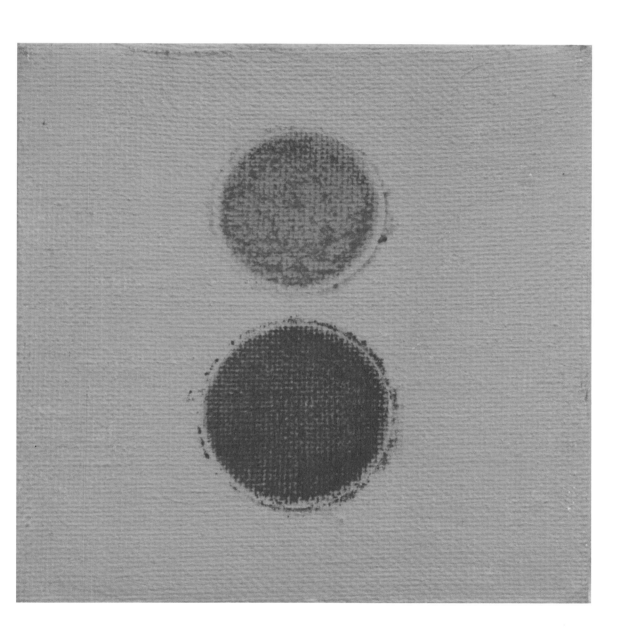

"Twin Moons #4"

6" x 6", Acrylic & Pastel

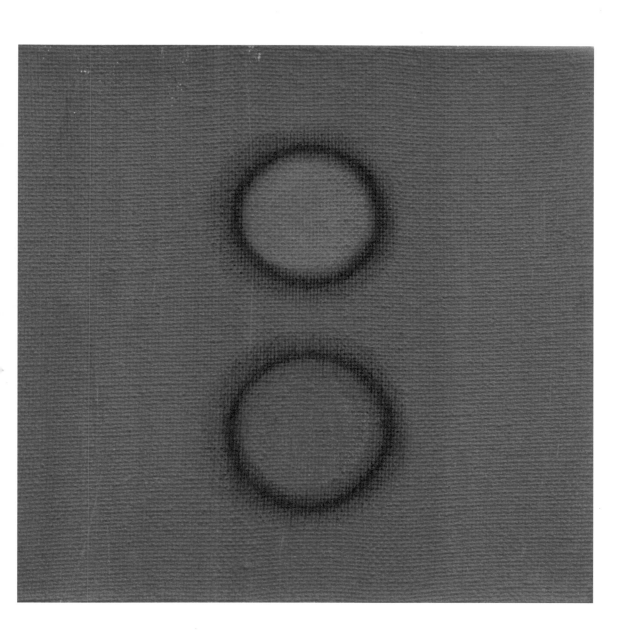

SECTION III

FAVORITE LIFE

I think about my favorite life,
whether I will ever inhabit it.

It must arrive without fanfare,
slipping into a room—bedroom,
kitchen, it makes little difference—
like a memory of who I once was
& of her, brushing out her hair,
curling into her jeans, a quick glance
at the clock on the dresser.

It was like that & perhaps
that life never really left.
Perhaps it is sitting alone
in the dark in a room
I've forgotten to enter.

CRY

The ever-crafty Talleyrand was often mistrusted by those he served. Yet Miles refused to sound hurried regardless of the tempo. How post-modern of you, quipped Nora, clearly tipsy. This is not the climate for crazy eyes. Some cats, nonetheless, will avoid certain species of mice. What swordsman indeed sired such vengeful blood? Turner reportedly retained his Cockney accent despite his growing acclaim. You may overlook the garlic rub if you wish. The subtle significance of a single interval. Wander or wonder? Sparkle or spackle? More than one merry olde soul is usually unnecessary. Murrow, however, later recalled the elderly Adolph Ochs as he first met him. The wistful joys of windows. The gratitude of doorways. The lyricism of high-backed chairs. I liked it better than I thought, she confided. While Bonnard continued to paint Marthe as a young woman even as she aged. *Ça digère toute ma vien.* His expression, although appropriately solemn, gave him a wicked look. Dommie D., she called, you'll get yourself all wet out there. It is safe, but it's safer elsewhere. From across the hallway, an infant's waking cry.

POEM ENDING WITH A QUESTION

In the country I live in
the sun burns through
the morning haze
like a blowtorch.

The grass, stunned
into submission, cries out
in a pale & withered voice.

By noon the air is sticky
as chewing gum in the mouths
of unruly children & those few
who brave the day proceed
like pack animals who, dreaming
of carrots, fear the whip.

Speech itself is hot to the touch.
What passes for a greeting
is just another word for *None.*

I tell you all this
so you will understand.

But do you?

DEFEAT

Concepts of beauty are of limited historical significance. It is not good to be too free, thought Pascal. They need more feathers, more sand, more mud. Greta, it seems, enjoys the fire, but not the smoke. He did not so much walk rapidly as charge toward us. No organic material, wood included, actually becomes stone. Will dangerous temptations subside of their own accord? Seconal or season-all? Scrivener or scavenger? Lizards have eyelids & ear openings; snakes, however, do not. While human emotions are both strange & familiar. The public be damned, believed Morgan. Go for it, he told her. Just go for it. A heart as capricious as a child's kite. The couple at the next table was talking such rot. Not sever, but severe. Not ferocious, but furious. There are no bears, brown or otherwise, among the rose bushes. The Eucharist, it appears, will not melt & must be chewed. What I don't want, Lauren stipulated, is to engender any tawdry knock-offs. *Qué cosa mas rara.* A laugh so startling passersby turned to look. At times, too much iridescence can get on one's nerves. One should never underestimate the difficulty of breaking a habit, no matter how nondescript. Pastel tones & feathery trees evoke a dreamy atmosphere. And yet a simple declarative sentence will suffice for now. Who among us, even in jest, has not spoken of defeat?

VERY VERY

Where am I ever going to find this again—
keepsake?, heirloom?, a bit of flashy trash?,
one may ask, you, in fact, might ask,
lowering the object, the thing, held in
your palm & raising it again—eye level?
or chest high?—assessing its heft.
A significant weight, a load proportionate
to its mass, is what you are after, as lightness,
for reasons not entirely rational, implies
a lack of seriousness, an absence of gravitas.
Desire itself, a yen or urge ratcheted up
by merely a dollop of fantasy, requires no set
time or preordained occasion. You could be
halted at a red light, monotony your only
companion, scanning the sidewalk
for a distraction. That is all that's nesting
in your hand at this moment, a distraction,
its presence noted, of indeterminate worth.
Cannot desire & progress coexist? Will not
a quick peek at a novel object engender
inner peace? Might not any sharpster,
slick as black ice on a two-lane, utilize
his sleight-of-hand to cause a shiny bauble
to vanish before your very very eyes?

EYES

Where populations are small, the distribution of power is relatively egalitarian. Most of the known universe, however, is either hydrogen or helium gas. The sundry details of O'Hara's daily round were a ready source of inspiration. Although appealing, blackmail was not in our immediate plans. I'm not one to shrug off coincidence, she protested, no matter how inopportune. Merely a slight change in barometric pressure is enough to set them off. Biedenbach habitually denied his intention to go cavorting around. The Commodore, incidentally, refused to answer his phone before it became fashionable. Confront or conflate? Connubial or convivial? The Mauryah empire extended as far south as what is now Karnataka. Mizener is sensitive to both Fitzgerald's limitations & his achievements. Hark, hooded ones, look to your souls. Who can tell us, they asked, whether that faint residue is significant? *Tiene límites pero no los conocemos.* With those who took such liberties I had little patience. Yet the number of cowboys who were junkies remains undetermined. Not noose, but news. Not Elsinore, but elsewhere. Aeschylus, it is certain, fought at Marathon & probably also at Salamis. A yellow flame indicates the gas isn't burning completely. Nevertheless, Eliza continued to be wary of certain field sports. The sensation isn't particularly painful, but I know it's there. Although they were of the same faith, they knew a different god. I ask you, what is a tiger without its stripes? What is a leopard without its spots? The restless grey bear of the wind in winter. If a good night's sleep were only a matter of lying down & shutting one's eyes.

ROAD MOVIE

Watching the road movie, you hope
it will never end. So much adventure,
you think, & even the breakdowns,
not entirely unexpected, seem
like fun. You wouldn't mind knowing
the evil characters, just not quite
so well. You realize someone you like
has to die. Halfway through, you begin
guessing who it will be & how.
You also wonder who the hero
really is. It may even be, since all this
is post-modern, the teenage girl;
so sweet & well-meaning, and smart, too,
though she may be showing a bit
more skin than is good for her
in the long run. Nevertheless, I am not
the hero, you conclude as the climax
jigsaws across the screen. Not here,
in this movie, nor anywhere else.

CRACK

The cruelty inherent in bear-baiting cannot be overestimated. Why bother setting the world on fire? I think artistically, contended Haims. Voodoo, some say, takes a back seat to hoodoo. Crabwise is merely an uncommon manner of walking. A child's knucklebone, if I'm not mistaken. Joyful birds, you, too, must forgive me. Alchemy or allergy? Pity or party? They proceeded into a spacious, light-filled room. Although there is nothing to be done about the fourteenth century. Please, do not let them steal your joy. A flat line will often appear to sag. What vultures have learned about humans. Mississippi, the entire state, remained a stumbling block. Yet they're through with five in Baltimore. Nuisances, of course, do have their value. He often thought of her. He thought of her often. Crack of dawn, my children. Crack of dawn.

HOTHOUSE

Tzara was Rosenstock
& E. Radnitsky, Lord knows why,
determined he was really Man Ray.
And let us not neglect Malcolm Little,
who was soon better known as Mr. X.

On the other hand,
Pound, of course, could be
no one other than Pound
& Hardy, mournful but spry
until the very end, certainly was.

The blind luck of the Anglo-Saxon
often passes unremarked.

What's in a name?, once queried
the most famous WASP of all,
whose interest in horticulture
appears confined to the stage.

The answer, if any, remains
delicate as a hothouse rose.

HOP

BB guns will not take down clouds no matter how large their pellets. The lessons of developed societies are clear, if not always obvious. All birds, unsurprisingly, can sense the slightest changes in air pressure. For the Robber Barons, any means of competition was justifiable. Invigorate me, pumpkin, she purred. I know you can. Exposure refers to the amount of light that falls on a negative. Perform or perfume? Syrup or stirrup? A whippet is also a small, fast tank. Gypsy kings are typically elderly, quarrelsome, & self-appointed. The cult of St. Cadillac always welcomes new members. I am waiting for my destiny to manifest itself, the salesclerk divulged, but I am becoming impatient. And yet Waldron's minimalist playing swings in a Monkish manner. Normally, a tree standing in the middle of a forest should not pose any problems. The printed message insisted that we shake well before using. Modern scholarship has added a 31st Dynasty to Monetho's original 30. I don't roll with pedestrian pursuits, she explained without rancor. While stark moonlight flooded the deserted square. The rigors of Crow life made the woman as capable as the men. Admonish, but not abolish. Shut, but not shunned. One may be pardoned for an undying love. Gaze thou no more into the bitter glass. You'll see, Spider will deny everything about Gashouse Striker. And claim he can't remember Copperhead Hop.

BIG DOGS

He spoke at length—even-voiced,
without blinking—about some big dogs
in the neighborhood, work dogs
no longer put to work & allowed
to roam wherever a fresh scent led them,
how he had talked to their owners,
how he was ready to put down one or two
of the more troublesome if it came to that.

By then some of us, having heard
enough, had looked away, yet others
remained attentive, their eyes locked
into that middle-distance stare,
hoping all the while to discover
the human being behind the disguise.

It was a fine afternoon, sunny
& mild, the woods at the property line
generously bestowing its green mercies
on the world, the closest neighbors
living down back roads a visitor
found only by accident or luck.

One night not long ago, Josh told us,
he was taking the curves of a back road
faster than he should when the front axle
of his pick-up snapped like a wishbone
& the truck careened into the trees.
A ditch halted his forward progress,
leaving him sitting there bruised

& battered but intact & cursing
the darkness to his heart's content.

We liked Josh's story better
but it was time to be heading home,
the day dimming like an old photograph,
& as we rose & turned, from across
the fields came the barking—
those oversized, mixed-breed shepherds
barking furiously, a half-dozen or more,
like artillery before an assault.

TEARS

October & the war was still there, but at a distance we could safely ignore. Yet certain talismans are useless against the darkness. And what if everything tastes like anger? I am really big on sparse, asserted Drager. All weather, he had heard somewhere, speaks its own language. Nineteen minutes, thirty-three seconds flashed onto the screen momentarily. In my mind, & there only, she was all January. Vanish or varnish? Bedside or bromide? Although Baker fled New York for Europe following his ninth arrest. The best teas come from the shoots of new leaves. Nonetheless, a terrible history looms over us. I am my shadow, she repeated. I am my shadow. Yet not a word from any of them, only a head shake or a nod. While the last stars tack across the night sky. Those long summer evenings walking the cane fields. Oft-told legends are often false, but not intentionally so. Everything I've said is accurate, lied Edson without hesitation. And just how many tears, approximately, must fall?

SEASON OF THE RAT

Sometime around midnight
I watched a rat saunter
across the parking lot, its time
belonging to no one but itself.

For all that—its silent, lazy nonchalance—
what I saw was a lean & bony creature,
& markedly so.

That much, alone in the dark,
was mine alone.

BREEZE

The repeated use of opioids will affect the brain's functions & structure. Generally, two trained body guards are considered a sufficient deterrent. I fear, sir, she responded modestly, you flatter me far more than I deserve. A vulture's wingspan endows it with exceptional lift. Some trees do not frown on alcoholic consumption. Some trees have a playful side they keep under wraps. The mark of the desert nomad's self-discipline is unmistakable. Moreover, the wide boulevards plotted by Huysmans allowed for unobstructed artillery fire. Siesta or sestina? Exit or exact? Noise, focused effectively, may become a voice. Nonetheless, Stanwyck, Dunne & Goddard had all been Follies girls. As a becalmed merchant clipper turned black in the noonday sun. Heating green malachite ore over a flame will bring forth copper. According to de Rotonchamp, Gauguin was an honest man who willingly paid his tailor. A candy cane is not a candle. A toupee is not a floor tile. So, he asked, is there anything that cries out to be included? The central feature of the wheel, however, is the fixed axle. All cuts sustained in sea water must be taken seriously. The poet, asserts Frye, cannot talk about what he knows. As yet, there is no preferred moment for an apocalypse. If there were any sort of breeze, it had precious little to say.

THE ODDS

for Arnold Gold, 1922-98

I am certain
that if I heckled you
long enough, chuckling sarcastically,
supplying a few particulars,
you would eventually recall
those final games of one-on-one,
the two of us alone
in that schoolyard in Rego Park.

You brought your A game that day,
the lickety-split moves
in the paint, the soft touch,
playing better than I'd seen
all winter & spring.

You took two-out-of-three
& I, somewhat bemused,
went off to my freshman year.

When I returned
basketball was no longer
a metaphor for things
I had yet to experience
or comprehend.

Older now
than you were
that afternoon, I admit
I thought about owning up

to not playing my hardest.

And as for you?
Well, what are the odds?

WHISKEY

Neanderthal graves provide the earliest evidence of ceremony. A show of wit may be an attempt to mask desperation. The beast is slightly tethered around its long, arching neck. There is darkness, she considered, & then there is the dark. Is mendacity, one wonders, the best policy? Now famous, Rothko feared that his paintings were merely fashionable. You may begin with black—a rich, velvety black—or finish with it. Piracy or privacy? Rubbish or rhubarb? His shoes, shined & stylish, were in perfect harmony. *Haben zie ein zimmer zu vermeiten?* There is more to witchcraft than possessing psychic powers. Upon approaching the border, read the scrawled note, you must become someone else. The stars footnoting the sky with their bright asterisks. Even in English, that compelling Yiddish syntax. Not titter, but teeter. Not perdition, but position. Wilde, asserted Years, spoke in a deliberately somnolent drawl. I'm sorry, but that one little gesture doesn't ring true. Yet know there are eyes upon you, vigilante in their watchfulness. One arm round a jar of whiskey, the other round my gal.

SENTINELS

About an hour before dusk
a small murder of crows swept down
behind the apartment blocks.

Seeking the uncluttered vistas
of the flat rooftops, the green cloisters
of the tall oaks & beeches,
they soon took their ease
on the high branches & unflappable
as hanging judges, surveyed
the expanse below.

One lone traveler touched ground
& probed the cracked & pitted asphalt,
its apricot beak pecking idly.
Glancing about, it swiveled its head
toward me now & then like a gun turret.

Everything around us
had gone still for a long moment,
the only sound the faint whistling
of a breeze through the leaves.

Yet with the next gust of wind
the single crow, its glossy wings
a perfect machine, rose & alighted
on a drainpipe while I remained
attentively in place, wide-eyed, mute
as a mannequin, just where it had
fixed me, sentinels, the both of us,
guarding a turning world.

POVERTY

The word tyrant only gradually became a term of reproach. Heroin, of course, was at first thought to be non-addictive. Who enjoys watching a small boat capsize during a sudden storm? I try to avoid border guards, he explained calmly. All borders, all guards. And yet rituals are an attempt to connect with the unknown. Goya's mature work was both Old Master & Modernist. She who was earth & water is now air & fire. Not sermon, but certain. Not federal, but folderol. The hammered anvil's gleeful, short-pitched ring. Each believes the axe will fall on someone else's neck. Lately, Solly has found refuge in trivial considerations. The true truth can be so boring, complained the Marquis. Most vaudeville comics traded in broad ethnic stereotypes. For the authentic tipi is always a tilted cone. One seldom hears Blanchard described as saintly. The ambiguity of the moment silenced everyone present. What is strange is wonderful, Nora concluded with a smile. Likewise, competitive wrestlers are explicitly forbidden from biting one another. A chalky feel indicates disintegration of the existing coating. Legacy or lunacy? Toronto or tornado? Modigliani preferred to sculpt in limestone when he could afford it. The red clay roads once common in Thailand have largely disappeared. Moreover, the place of honor is always directly opposite the entranceway. You were so wise, duckie, to choose another destination, the Matron concurred cheerily. The condor, the crocodile, the wolf-headed god. His answer as thoughtless as taking a breath. I no longer fear poverty or death, attested the exiled Machiavelli in a letter to a friend.

WATERMAN

His forearms are the color
of red clay, but beefier.
Out on the water all my life,
he avows, while I think of
the cautionary tales of old hands,
of a bad ending someday,
keeping my misgivings to myself.

He'd been offered more than
a million for acreage fronting
the bay, yet wouldn't budge.
Where would I go?, he laughs.
All the real crabbing is right here.

Drifting off, I envision those hordes
of hipsters, their pale limbs
resplendent with inked symbols
arcane as ancient codes, waiting
for a key to unlock their lives.

Here & now, the outboard motor
churns the surf into a frothy wake
as my companion leans into
the work, his bare arms, sun-baked
as bricks, bending to their tasks.

DANCING

Honesty sessions are not as much fun as some believe. Melancholy, it is said, is the dark side of genius. Such anatomy may have been improvised on the spot. The dim hideaways in which ghosts lurk. While herds of bison followed fixed routes across the Great Plains. One may readily determine whether an object is round or not. What Haims knows about Chile has little to do with climate. Pursue or persist? Fixture or future? It was more of a mood, really, than an attitude. The murmurs of porchfront conversations dappling the night air. Neither peaches nor petticoats are intended to frighten small children. Does gravity ever fail us? A medieval freeman, however, could expect compensation for personal injury. It was a noise, sure, but a quiet noise. Here & there a man raised his head & shoulders above the murky floodwaters. Must the bitter always accompany the sweet? I am still wary of dancing, disclosed Allison, with respectable people.

PERFECT DAY

For Kathleen Wheaton

Some years back I saw a hog slaughtered,
home-style, in the backyard of a small house
on the outskirts of a small town in Piedmont Virginia.
The hog itself took its bullet in a spot the size
of a dime right above its eyes & died almost bloodlessly,
slumping down in the trough where its carcass was then
boiled so that the thick bristles could be easily scrapped off
& the business of country butchering could proceed.

I was among a fair-sized crowd, locals mainly,
who stood watching while a few men did all the work.
Nothing much was said—this was no undertaking
for nonsense—except for the occasional polite
but terse directive or encouraging epithet or two.
It was early, an overcast fall morning chilly enough
to numb your hands & feet if you didn't keep moving,
stomping & stepping in place like a buckdancer.
The perfect day, agreed everyone, their words
ballooning into instant puffs of mist.

It didn't take long & as you may have guessed
I haven't returned since, but whenever I unfold
my creased road map of Virgina & look it over
I can't miss it—that quiet little town, the red X
where I'd marked it throbbing like a wound.

"Emerald Canyon"

12" x 12", Acrylic

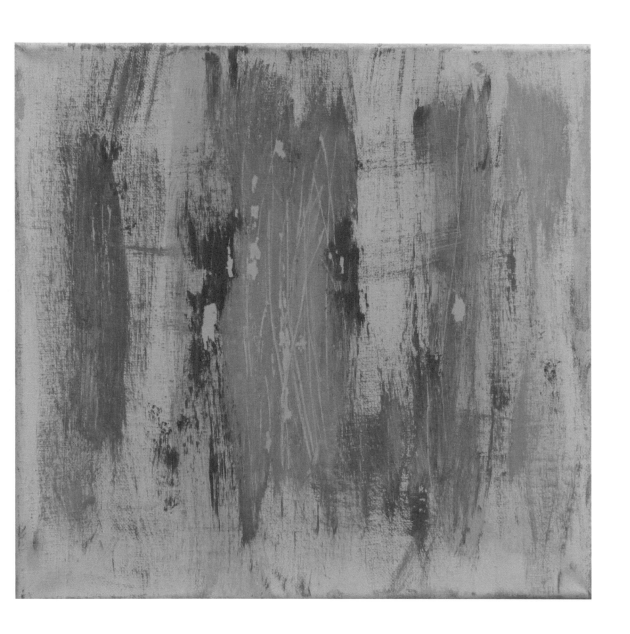

"Destination #2"

5" x 5", Acrylic & Pastel

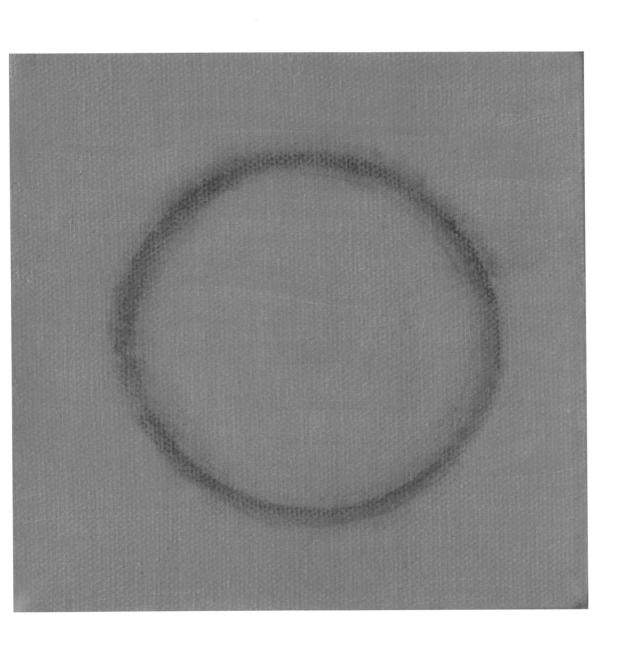

"Undiscovered Planets"

10" x 8", Acrylic & Pastel

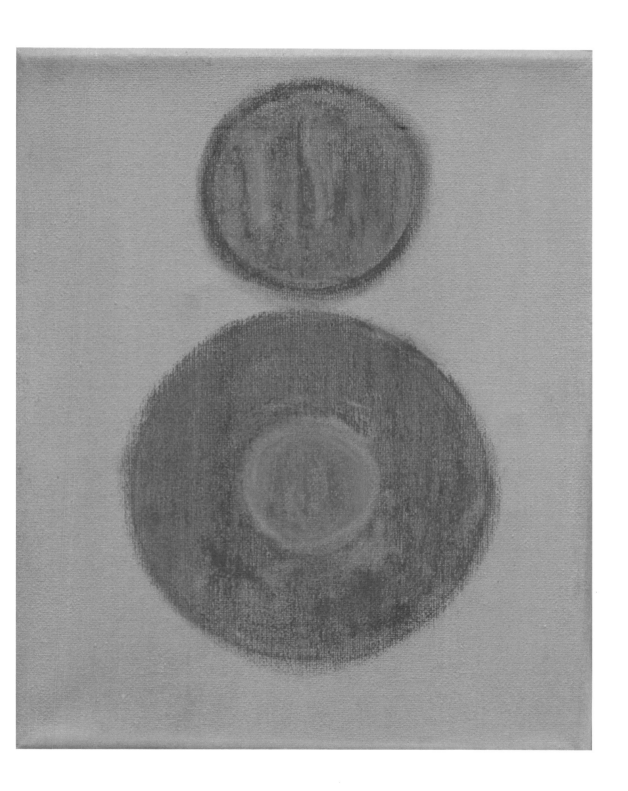

99

About The Author

Photo Credit: Jessica Lynn Dotson

Sid Gold is the author of four previous collections: *Working Vocabulary* (Washington Writers' Publishing House, 1997 & 2021), *The Year of the Dog Throwers* (Broadkill River Press, 2010), *Good With Oranges* (Broadkill River Press, 2015) and *Crooked Speech* (Pond Road Press, 2018). He is a twice recipient of the Maryland State Art Council Individual Artist Award for Poetry and in 2019 he was voted among Baltimore's Best Poets in the Baltimore Magazine Reader's Poll. His poems have appeared in reviews, journals and anthologies for more than forty years. A native New Yorker, he has lived in Hyattsville, Maryland, for a number of years.

Graphic Designer Biography

Sanket Patel is an experienced 33 year old graphic designer, illustrator and web designer from Groton, Connecticut. Born in India and moving to the States at age five. He developed a strong appreciation for cultures of both Indian and the United States. His style as an artist incorporates his Indian roots and expresses this culture it in a modern and innovative way. With several years of experience working in a multitude of design roles and settings, Sanket has become a very sought after designer and is able to bring a creative yet professional approach to any project.

Printed in the USA
CPSIA information can be obtained
at www.ICGtesting.com
JSHW040833241023
50724JS00002B/11